MAYER SMITH

The Billionaire's Double Life

Contents

One

The Perfect Escape

Isabelle Stone stared out the private jet's window, watching the vast expanse of blue sky stretch endlessly beneath her. The sun hovered low, casting a warm glow on the clouds. The noise of the engines hummed softly in the background, but her thoughts were far from the tranquil scenery outside. It had been hours since she left the shimmering skyline of New York, hours since she'd stepped out of her life—her real life—into something entirely unknown. And yet, the overwhelming sensation was not one of excitement or freedom, but of suffocating guilt.

For the past year, Isabelle had been leading a double life. The world knew her as the heiress to the Stone Hotel empire, the glamorous daughter of an infamous business magnate. She was constantly photographed at charity galas, spotted at the latest fashion shows, and caught in the high-profile world of luxury.

But behind every glittering smile was a woman suffocating under the weight of expectations, of obligations she never signed up for. The truth was, Isabelle hated her life.

She had been raised to lead the family business, her future mapped out with a precision that left no room for deviation. When her father, a formidable hotel magnate, had passed away, the responsibility fell squarely on her shoulders. At first, she had embraced it—at least she thought she did. She enjoyed the power, the endless meetings, the executive decisions, but it wasn't long before she began to feel the crushing loneliness of it all. No one saw the real Isabelle Stone. They only saw the brand.

And so, when the pressure reached unbearable heights, when the cameras started to follow her every move, when the mansion seemed more like a prison than a home, Isabelle made a decision. She was going to disappear.

The plan had been years in the making, though no one—not even her closest friends or staff—had any idea. Isabelle had meticulously crafted her escape, arranging everything with the precision of a professional. She created a fake travel blog, designing a persona that was as different from her real self as possible. She called herself Izzy Bloom, a quirky, adventurous young woman who traveled the world with a camera in hand and a story to tell. It was a far cry from the polished, poised heiress people thought they knew. But it was the only way she could break free from the life that had been handed to her.

The jet was on its final descent, and the reality of what she was doing was beginning to sink in. This was it. She had crossed the point of no return. No more business calls, no more press interviews, no more appearances. Isabelle Stone, the heiress, would cease to exist for as long as she chose. She, Izzy Bloom, would be free.

As the jet landed with a soft thud, Isabelle's chest tightened. There would be no turning back now. She glanced around the luxurious cabin, where plush seats and polished wood exuded wealth and opulence. This was the last time she would experience this kind of indulgence, the last time she would enjoy the comfort of her family's money.

The moment the plane came to a stop, Isabelle quickly gathered her belongings. She wore a simple, unremarkable dress— light denim with a loose-fitting style—something far less conspicuous than the high-fashion outfits she'd been known to wear. She tucked her long, golden hair under a floppy hat and put on large, round sunglasses that covered most of her face. There was no time to waste. The airport terminal was waiting, and so was her new life.

Stepping off the jet and onto the tarmac, the heat hit her immediately. The air was thick and warm, the kind of sticky heat that made you sweat from the moment you stepped outside. Isabelle had chosen her destination carefully—an exotic island off the coast of Thailand, a place far removed from the glitz and glam of her New York life. Here, no one would recognize her. No one would know that she was the daughter of one of the world's wealthiest men.

She made her way through the airport, her heart pounding with each step. For a moment, she wondered if she had made a mistake. What if someone recognized her? What if someone tracked her down? But those thoughts quickly dissipated as she stepped out into the bustling street, her senses assaulted by the sounds of honking taxis, the shouts of street vendors, and the overwhelming scent of spices and street food. The chaos felt liberating. For the first time in years, Isabelle felt alive.

She had arranged everything in advance—her accommodations, the local contacts who would help her navigate the unfamiliar surroundings. It had all been set up. But there was still the lingering fear, the fear of being found, of being dragged back into the life she was so desperate to escape. She had no choice but to keep moving forward.

As Isabelle checked into her modest hotel, she couldn't help but notice the stark contrast to the opulent hotels she was used to. The lobby was small and unassuming, with a few tourists lounging on mismatched sofas. The staff greeted her with warm smiles, but it was nothing like the impersonal, luxury-service world she had come from. Here, she felt like a person, not a brand.

She made her way to her room, a simple space with a small balcony overlooking the busy street below. As she unpacked, the unease started to creep back in. What was she really doing here? Could she really leave everything behind? What if her family found out? What would they think? But she had to silence those thoughts. She was Izzy Bloom now, and she had no intention of going back.

As night fell, Isabelle sat on the balcony, the warm breeze rustling her hair. The city was alive with sounds, but she felt a strange emptiness. She was free—so why didn't it feel like it?

The next morning, she began her new routine. She explored the streets, documenting everything through her camera lens, uploading photos to her travel blog. Her online followers began to grow, intrigued by the mysterious Izzy Bloom. The excitement of creating something new, of being someone new, thrilled her. She was no longer the polished heiress, the woman who lived in a gilded cage. She was just a girl, walking the streets of a foreign land, discovering the world for the first time.

But as the days passed, Isabelle couldn't shake the feeling that something was missing. For all the freedom she had gained, for all the adventure she was experiencing, there was a hollowness inside her—a sense that she was still searching for something she couldn't quite name. She had everything she ever wanted… or so she thought. But as she roamed the markets, the streets, and the remote villages, she began to realize that the world she was exploring was nothing like the one she had left behind.

And then, one evening, as she wandered down a quiet alleyway, she saw him—Alex Rivers. He was leaning against a weathered brick wall, his camera hanging from his neck, capturing the fading light of the setting sun. There was something magnetic about him—something that made Isabelle pause in her tracks. He looked nothing like the polished men she was used to. He was rugged, his clothes worn and torn, his hair a mess of curls, but there was an undeniable presence about him. His eyes locked with hers for a brief moment, and in that instant, she felt something shift inside her.

For the first time since her escape, Isabelle felt something more than the pull of her old life. She felt the stirrings of curiosity, of something unknown. She had no idea how, but she knew that meeting Alex Rivers would change everything.

Her perfect escape, it seemed, was just beginning.

Two

A New Identity

⁂

Isabelle awoke to the sound of the bustling market below her hotel balcony, the faint clamor of street vendors haggling with tourists drifting up through the open window. She sat up, her head foggy from a restless night, the reality of her escape still settling in. It had only been a few days since she had stepped away from her world of luxury, but already she felt the tension begin to dissolve, as though the weight of her past was slowly lifting.

She reached for her phone on the nightstand, the glow of the screen briefly lighting up the dim room. The familiar notifications were there—messages from her personal assistant, news alerts about the latest developments in the Stone Hotel empire, and, most unsettling, an email from her father's lawyer. But Isabelle wasn't ready to deal with any of it. Not today.

She quickly swiped the notifications away, closing the phone with a sigh. It was too soon. She had not yet found herself in this new life she had created, and the shadows of her old life still loomed over her. She had crafted the perfect disguise, built an entirely new persona, but deep down, Isabelle knew she was only fooling herself. No matter how far she traveled or how many times she used the alias "Izzy Bloom," she could never fully escape the life that had been thrust upon her.

But today was different. Today, she had a new mission, a new goal to focus on—one she could not afford to neglect.

She stood up, stretched, and took a deep breath, allowing the air to fill her lungs. It smelled different here, heavier with the scent of spices and the unmistakable tang of humidity. The chaos outside was foreign and overwhelming, but in it, she felt alive. This was the freedom she had craved for so long.

After a quick breakfast of fresh fruit and coconut water, she set to work. Izzy Bloom's travel blog needed updating. She had been documenting every moment since her arrival, from the colorful streets of Bangkok to the serene beaches of Koh Phi Phi. She'd quickly gained a modest following, some intrigued by her bold approach to travel, others perhaps merely attracted to the mystery of her identity. Either way, the attention was enough to give her a sense of purpose—a sense of belonging that had been sorely lacking in her life before.

The anonymity was intoxicating. Izzy Bloom was someone new—someone with no expectations, no responsibilities, no legacy to uphold. She could be whoever she wanted to be. And yet, as she clicked through her photos, selecting the ones that captured the essence of her journey, a wave of doubt crashed over her. Was she simply running away? Was this truly the life she wanted, or was it an illusion, a temporary escape from a world she could never truly leave behind?

She dismissed the thought, focusing on the task at hand. There was no going back now. She had made her choice.

As she continued to upload photos and write about her adventures, the day passed in a blur. The sun dipped low in the sky, casting a warm golden light over the city as Isabelle—or rather, Izzy—decided to explore the streets for the evening. Her latest post had garnered more attention than she'd anticipated, and the comments began rolling in, some asking for tips on the best places to visit, others commenting on her striking photos of the local culture. It was clear that her followers were invested in her journey.

She left her room and descended the narrow stairwell, stepping out onto the busy street. The energy of the city wrapped around her like a warm embrace, its pulse quickening as people moved about with purpose. Motorbikes zoomed past, their drivers weaving through traffic with deft skill, while pedestrians haggled with vendors selling everything from fresh fruit to handcrafted jewelry. The smell of grilled meats and sizzling spices filled the air, making her stomach growl.

Her eyes scanned the crowd, taking in the vibrant colors of the stalls and the diversity of the people who had gathered. In this place, she was just another face in the crowd, a foreigner in a world of strangers. No one looked at her twice, and that was exactly what she wanted.

As she wandered through the market, her camera slung casually over her shoulder, Isabelle felt the familiar tug of uncertainty. She was free, yes, but there was an undercurrent of discomfort that she couldn't shake. She missed the structure of her old life, the stability, even the expectations that came with being part of a powerful family. Here, on the streets of Thailand, she was unmoored, drifting without purpose.

Her phone buzzed, snapping her out of her reverie. She glanced at the screen, seeing a message from one of her old friends from New York. The message was brief, but the words stung like a slap.

"Where are you, Izzy? The Stones are worried. Call us."

The message made her stomach tighten, but she quickly dismissed it. She had known the risks when she left, and no amount of text messages could undo her decision. Her family, her business—those were things she no longer wanted to be tethered to. They had their life, and she would have hers.

Her gaze drifted back to the bustling streets, and that's when she saw him again.

Alex Rivers.

He was standing across the street, leaning against a faded building, the sun casting a golden halo around his figure. He was the same man she had seen earlier, the rugged photographer who had caught her attention at the market just days before. He seemed to be studying the scene before him through the lens of his camera, the way he moved so effortlessly among the chaos, as though he had lived here his entire life.

Curiosity gnawed at her. She had never been one to approach strangers, especially not someone like him. He was everything she wasn't—raw, untamed, unpolished. Isabelle had been born into privilege, raised with everything she could ever want, but here was Alex, living a life that was entirely foreign to her, a life she could never truly understand. And yet, there was something magnetic about him.

Her feet carried her toward him without thinking. The crowd around her seemed to fade away as she neared the photographer, her heart pounding in her chest.

"Alex," she said, the words coming out more nervously than she had intended.

He looked up, his intense eyes locking with hers, and for a moment, the world seemed to stop. His lips curved into a small, knowing smile, and his gaze softened. "Izzy, right?"

"Actually, it's Isabelle," she replied, her voice a little too high. She instantly regretted it, but it was too late to take it back. She had already introduced herself as Izzy, the name she had carefully crafted to avoid suspicion, to become someone else.

"Isabelle," he repeated, his tone thoughtful. "What brings you to this side of town?"

"I was exploring," she said, trying to sound casual, but the unease in her voice betrayed her. "This place is incredible. I'm documenting my travels." She gestured vaguely toward the camera hanging at her side.

"Ah, another traveler," he said with a slight chuckle. "But you don't look like a tourist. I've been around, seen many people come through here, but there's something about you. You don't quite fit in."

Isabelle tensed. "I'm not a tourist. I'm… just traveling. For a while."

"Not running away, I hope?" he asked, his gaze piercing. There was something in his eyes, a hint of understanding, as if he knew exactly why she was here, why she was hiding in plain sight.

The question caught her off guard. "I—" She hesitated, unsure of how to respond. How could she explain why she'd left everything behind? Why she had chosen this life of uncertainty?

Alex studied her for a long moment, as though waiting for an answer that she wasn't ready to give. Finally, he spoke again, his voice softer this time. "If you're looking for something, maybe I can help. I know this city better than most. There's more to see here than you might think."

For a fleeting moment, Isabelle considered his offer. She didn't know what she was looking for, not really. But she did know that something in her had shifted since she arrived, something that kept drawing her to this man, to his free-spirited way of life.

"Maybe you can," she said, the words escaping her before she could stop them.

And just like that, the uncertainty that had plagued her began to fade. In Alex, she saw not just a stranger, but someone who might just offer her a glimpse of the life she had been searching for.

And so, Isabelle's new identity began to take shape—not just in the blog, not just in the photos, but in the choices she made, in the people she met, and in the way she allowed herself to be seen.

The journey she thought she had begun was only just beginning.

Three

The Encounter

Isabelle wasn't sure what had drawn her to Alex. It wasn't just his rugged, unkempt appearance or the way he carried himself as though the world didn't quite belong to him. It wasn't even the fact that he had seemed to know something about her without saying a word—something about her restlessness, her desire to break free. No, it was more than that. It was the way he made her feel, the inexplicable tug in her chest when their eyes met, as though everything she had been running from had led her to this very moment.

After their brief exchange outside the market, Alex had suggested they go for a walk, guiding her away from the crowded streets and into a quieter part of the city. Isabelle hadn't even hesitated, too curious to resist. As they walked, he spoke casually about the places he'd visited, the people he'd met, and the stories he'd captured through the lens of his camera. His voice was rich, full of life, and there was something magnetic about the way he spoke.

"You can't really know a place until you've walked its streets, until you've sat with the locals, heard their stories," Alex said as they passed a street-side café where an elderly couple sat sipping tea. "Most tourists just skim the surface, capture the postcard shots, and leave. But there's so much more beneath the surface."

Isabelle nodded, pretending to follow his words, but inside, she was distracted. There was an undeniable sense of familiarity in the way he spoke, an honesty she hadn't encountered in years. She had spent her life around people who spoke in carefully crafted sentences, each word weighed with intent, each gesture measured. Alex, on the other hand, was raw. Unfiltered. And for the first time in what felt like forever, Isabelle was drawn to it.

"Have you always lived like this?" she asked, her voice betraying more curiosity than she intended. She wasn't sure why she had asked the question—she didn't even know what answer she was hoping for.

Alex gave a small chuckle, his eyes scanning the street ahead. "Lived like what? Free? It's not a choice you make one day; it's just the way things happen. I don't think anyone really plans to live like this. Life just takes you down paths you didn't expect."

There was an enigmatic quality about him, something she couldn't quite place. Perhaps it was the uncertainty in his tone, the way his words seemed to carry a deeper meaning. It wasn't just that he had lived in places she could only dream of visiting—it was the life he had lived there, the choices he had made, and the stories he had to tell.

They walked for what felt like hours, until the crowded streets began to thin out, and the sounds of the city faded into the background. The sun had started its descent, casting long shadows across the pavement. Isabelle felt herself becoming increasingly aware of the distance between her and her former life. The city was so different from the sleek, fast-paced world she had left behind. Here, time seemed to slow down, and people lived in the moment.

Eventually, Alex led her to a small, tucked-away café, its wooden tables lined with potted plants. The place was quiet, with only a few locals scattered around, sipping coffee or engaging in quiet conversation. Isabelle sat at one of the tables with him, her hands folded in her lap as she took in the warm atmosphere.

"You'll find that the best conversations happen in places like this," Alex said, ordering two cups of black coffee from the waitress who arrived moments later. "Tourists come, take their photos, and leave. But the real magic is in the conversations, the stories that are shared."

She nodded, grateful for the calmness of the moment. But despite the tranquil setting, her mind was racing. She was still adjusting to this new world—one without the watchful eyes of the press, one without the constant chatter of her public life. But being here, in this quiet corner of the world, felt like an almost uncomfortable freedom. It was like stepping out of a costume, only to realize that you weren't quite sure who you were beneath it.

Alex leaned back in his chair, his eyes studying her intently. "You know," he said after a long pause, "I can tell you're not really here for the adventure. Not the way you think you are."

The words hit her like a punch to the gut. Isabelle froze, unsure of how to respond. Her mouth went dry, and she swallowed nervously, trying to brush off the feeling of being caught.

"What do you mean?" she asked, forcing a casualness she didn't feel.

Alex gave a half-smile, a knowing look crossing his face. "You're running away," he said, his voice low, almost gentle. "I can see it in the way you move, the way you talk, like you're trying to outrun something. But I don't think you know what that something is yet."

Isabelle's breath caught in her throat. She had been so careful, so deliberate in crafting her new persona. How could he see through it so easily? She was Izzy Bloom, the carefree travel blogger with no past, no history, and no obligations. She had made sure of it. And yet, sitting here in this quiet café with Alex, she felt like an open book, her pages exposed, her secrets laid bare.

She tried to regain control, her mind scrambling for a response. "I'm not running away," she said, her voice tight. "I'm just…

exploring. I'm taking a break from my normal life."

Alex raised an eyebrow, his gaze piercing. "Normal life? You don't know what normal is, do you? Normal for you is a life of luxury, with everything handed to you on a silver platter. But that's not what the world is like for most people. You can't just pick up and leave when things get tough, Isabelle. The real world doesn't work that way."

The sting of his words hit harder than she expected. There was a truth in them, one she didn't want to acknowledge. He was right. The world she came from was one of privilege and control. She had never had to struggle the way most people did. Everything was arranged for her. Her future was decided long before she was even born. And now, here she was, pretending to be someone else, trying to escape the life that had been thrust upon her. But could she really leave it all behind? Could she truly step into this new world Alex was offering her?

"I don't know what you want me to say," Isabelle said, her voice trembling slightly. "I'm just trying to figure things out. I'm not asking for your judgment."

Alex's expression softened, and for a brief moment, Isabelle saw a flicker of something more compassionate in his eyes. "I'm not judging you," he said quietly. "I'm just telling you that running away won't solve anything. You have to face it, eventually. Whatever it is you're running from."

The words hung in the air between them, heavy with meaning. Isabelle felt a lump form in her throat, the pressure of everything she had been trying to ignore starting to build inside her. What was she running from? Was it really her family? The hotel empire? The life that had been planned for her? Or was it something deeper, something that had been buried inside her for years?

Before she could respond, the waitress returned with their coffees, placing the steaming mugs in front of them. Isabelle wrapped her fingers around the warm cup, seeking comfort in its heat.

Alex was quiet for a moment, sipping his coffee before speaking again. "You know, I've traveled the world, met all kinds of people. But there's always something that brings you back to the same place. Whatever it is you're running from, it'll follow you until you face it."

His words seemed to resonate in the silence between them. Isabelle's thoughts swirled, her heart beating faster, as though something within her was beginning to crack open. She wasn't sure what was happening—what Alex had said, what she had been feeling—but something had shifted.

She didn't know if she was ready to face whatever was haunting her, but for the first time, she wasn't sure she could keep running. Not anymore.

The encounter, it seemed, had only just begun. And the journey she thought she had started would soon take a turn that would change everything.

Four

Behind the Lens

The days that followed were a blur. Isabelle—Izzy Bloom, as she now called herself—had grown accustomed to this new routine, this new identity. Her life was no longer dominated by the rigid schedules of luxury and status. She spent her days wandering through markets, capturing images of the world with the camera Alex had handed her, while the world of high society faded further into the distance. Every morning, she donned a new persona, one that belonged to the carefree traveler, free of the expectations that had weighed on her shoulders for so long. But beneath it all, there was a creeping sensation of unease, a sense that she was always just one step away from being caught, from being forced back into a world she had no desire to return to.

The bright afternoon sun cast long shadows across the street as Isabelle walked beside Alex, her feet carrying her across uneven cobblestone streets, the camera dangling loosely from her neck. She had become more skilled with it in the last few days, her fingers instinctively finding the right angles, capturing the fleeting moments of beauty that most people overlooked. Alex had taught her how to focus not just on the scene before her but on the emotion behind it—the joy of a child playing in the street, the quiet sorrow of an old man sitting alone at a café, the energy of a market in full swing. Each photograph felt like a story, a piece of the world she could never have fully understood before.

But with each click of the camera, Isabelle felt herself becoming more immersed in this strange new life. Alex had become more than just a guide; he had become her anchor. He was teaching her how to see the world through his lens, a perspective she had never thought to adopt. And with every new day, she found herself falling deeper into the life he led—the life of a wanderer, a photographer who lived on the fringes, capturing moments of beauty and despair with equal ease.

Today, however, felt different. There was an electricity in the air, a tension that Isabelle couldn't quite place. They had set out early that morning to explore a hidden temple, deep in the heart of the jungle, far from the typical tourist spots. It was a place Alex had spoken of with reverence, a place where the history of the land seemed to linger in the air, thick with mystery and the weight of centuries past. Isabelle had been both excited and nervous about the trip, but Alex's enthusiasm had been infectious, and she had agreed without hesitation.

As they neared the entrance to the temple, the atmosphere

shifted. The jungle was dense, the air heavy with humidity, and the only sounds were the occasional chirping of birds and the rustling of leaves underfoot. Alex led the way, his steps confident and sure as he navigated the overgrown path. Isabelle followed closely behind, her breath quickening with each step. The jungle seemed to close in around them, the trees towering above like silent sentinels, casting deep shadows across the ground.

"Here it is," Alex said, his voice barely above a whisper, as they reached the entrance to the temple. The stone structure loomed before them, partially obscured by the thick vines and foliage that had overtaken it over the centuries. The walls were covered in intricate carvings, the figures worn and eroded by time, but still unmistakably telling the story of a forgotten civilization.

Isabelle felt a shiver run down her spine as she stepped closer, her eyes tracing the ancient symbols etched into the stone. There was something haunting about the place, something that felt wrong, as though the temple itself were alive, watching them. She could feel the weight of history pressing in on her, a feeling she had never experienced before.

Alex, however, was already inside, his camera raised to capture the grandeur of the temple's interior. Isabelle hesitated at the threshold, her heart pounding in her chest. She had always been drawn to beauty, but this was something different. This was not the polished luxury of her old life, not the carefully curated images of travel brochures. This was raw, untamed, and unsettling in its quiet majesty.

"Come on," Alex called from inside, his voice echoing through the stone chamber. "You'll want to see this."

With a deep breath, Isabelle stepped into the temple, the cool air inside sending a shiver through her. The interior was even more breathtaking than she had imagined, the stone walls covered in faded murals that told the story of a long-forgotten culture. She moved closer to one of the murals, her fingers lightly brushing the surface, tracing the outline of a figure—a woman, her face half-obscured by time, her eyes staring out from the stone as though she could see Isabelle standing there.

Alex was already moving through the temple, his camera clicking away, capturing each new angle with a precision that seemed almost mechanical. Isabelle followed him, but her mind was elsewhere, lost in the mystery of the place. There was something about it, something that gnawed at her. The silence of the temple felt oppressive, as though it were holding its breath, waiting for something.

She couldn't shake the feeling that they were being watched. The hairs on the back of her neck prickled, and she turned around, half-expecting to see someone standing behind her. But there was no one. The temple was empty, save for the two of them. Still, the sensation lingered.

"Are you okay?" Alex asked, his voice breaking through her thoughts. He was standing by a set of ancient stairs, his camera lowered as he watched her closely. His eyes narrowed slightly, a look of concern crossing his features.

"Yeah," Isabelle replied, forcing a smile. "Just… this place feels strange."

Alex gave a small nod, his lips quirking into a smile. "It has that effect on people. It's like the past never really leaves places like this. You can feel it, can't you?"

Isabelle didn't answer. She couldn't explain it, couldn't put the feeling into words, but she nodded anyway. She could feel it, yes—something in the air, something that pulsed with the rhythm of the temple's forgotten history. It was as though the very stones of the place were alive, breathing with the weight of centuries of secrets.

Alex moved to the base of the stairs, crouching down to inspect something hidden beneath the stone. Isabelle's curiosity got the better of her, and she walked over to him, her eyes scanning the ground as she approached.

"What is it?" she asked, her voice barely above a whisper.

Alex didn't answer immediately. His hands moved carefully, brushing away the dust and debris that had accumulated over the years. Finally, he reached something solid—an object half-buried beneath the stone. With a grunt, he pulled it free, revealing a small, intricately carved box. It was made of dark wood, the surface covered in delicate patterns that Isabelle didn't recognize. She knelt down beside him, her fingers brushing the box as she examined it.

"Where did this come from?" Isabelle asked, her voice trembling slightly as she took in the strange object. The box felt oddly warm to the touch, as though it had been hidden here for centuries, waiting to be discovered.

"I don't know," Alex replied, his voice quiet as he turned the box over in his hands. "I've never seen anything like it before. But there's something about it… something strange."

Isabelle's heart skipped a beat as she looked at the box. There was something undeniably eerie about it, something that tugged at the edges of her memory, but she couldn't place it. She had never been particularly superstitious, but in this moment, surrounded by the ancient walls of the temple, she couldn't shake the feeling that they had uncovered something they weren't meant to find.

Alex's eyes were fixed on the box, his expression unreadable. "We should take it with us," he said after a long pause, his voice filled with a strange intensity. "It might be worth something— something important."

Isabelle hesitated. There was a voice in her head telling her not to touch it, telling her to leave it where it was, but Alex's gaze was fixed on her now, his eyes imploring, as though he needed her agreement. And so, against her better judgment, she nodded.

"Okay," she said, her voice soft. "Let's take it."

But as Alex carefully placed the box into his backpack, Isabelle couldn't shake the feeling that they had just crossed a line. The weight of the box, now resting beside her, felt oppressive, as though it carried the weight of the temple itself.

They left the temple soon after, the oppressive atmosphere still clinging to them as they made their way back down the narrow path. The jungle seemed darker now, as if it had sensed the disturbance. Isabelle's heart beat faster with each step, her mind racing with questions she couldn't answer.

Had they just discovered something ancient, something lost to history? Or had they unearthed something better left buried, a secret that the temple had kept hidden for a reason?

Isabelle wasn't sure, but one thing was clear—whatever the box contained, it was about to change everything.

And she wasn't sure if she was ready for that.

Five

The Spark of Doubt

I sabelle stood at the edge of the beach, her toes digging into the warm sand, the sound of crashing waves filling her ears. The sun had just descended, casting a soft golden glow across the water. It was a beautiful sight she had seen countless times in her travels, yet today, it felt different. The waves seemed to mirror her thoughts—constant, crashing, swirling, never truly still. She couldn't shake the nagging feeling that had taken root in her chest.

For the past few weeks, everything had felt like a dream. The freedom. The anonymity. The sense of possibility that came with being Izzy Bloom, the carefree travel blogger who could go anywhere and do anything. She had left her father's world behind, distancing herself from the cold, calculated luxury of the Stone family legacy. And for a while, it had felt right. It had felt like a fresh start—a way to rediscover who she was, away from the pressure of being who everyone else expected her to be.

But now, as she watched the waves crash against the shore, a new feeling settled over her—doubt. It crept in like the tide, soft at first, but now unrelenting. What was she really running from? Was it just the weight of her family's expectations, or was it something deeper, something within herself that she had yet to face?

"You've been quiet lately," Alex's voice broke through her thoughts, his footsteps soft in the sand behind her.

Isabelle turned to see him walking toward her, his camera slung over his shoulder. He had always been a quiet presence in her life, but today, there was something different in the way he watched her. It was as if he could sense the shift in her energy, the growing unease that had begun to shadow her every step.

"I'm just thinking," she said, forcing a smile as she turned back to the ocean. "About everything. About where I'm going next."

Alex didn't respond immediately. He simply stood beside her, his gaze fixed on the horizon. The wind tugged at his hair, the same wind that tousled Isabelle's own hair. For a moment, they stood in silence, the only sound the distant call of seabirds and the rhythmic crash of the waves.

"You're not really sure, are you?" Alex asked finally, his voice soft but direct.

Isabelle's stomach tightened. She wanted to deny it, to brush it off and pretend that everything was fine, that she had it all figured out. But she knew he was right. She wasn't sure. Not anymore.

"I don't know," she admitted, her voice barely above a whisper. "I thought I did. I thought I was doing the right thing, leaving everything behind, starting over. But now… now it feels like I'm not really running toward something. I'm just running away."

Alex turned to face her, his expression unreadable. "Running from what?"

She glanced at him, his eyes soft but intense. They had spent days together, shared stories, shared laughter, and even moments of quiet understanding, but in this moment, Isabelle felt a distance between them. She wasn't sure if it was the doubt gnawing at her insides or the realization that Alex might be the one person who truly saw her—who could see through the facade she had built for herself.

"I don't know what I'm running from," she said, her voice breaking. "Maybe it's just… everything. The expectations, the pressure, the life that was chosen for me before I even knew what it was like to make my own choices. I thought that if I left it all behind, I could finally breathe. But I don't know if I can just erase who I was, who they made me be."

Alex's gaze softened, and he stepped closer to her, his presence comforting yet slightly overwhelming. "You don't have to erase who you were, Isabelle. But you do have to decide who you want to be. The only way to stop running is to face what you're running from. You can't keep hiding forever."

His words hit her harder than she expected. They were simple, but they were true. Isabelle had spent so much of her life running—first from the confines of her family's empire, then from the weight of expectations, and now, from the person she was becoming. She had believed that the further she ran, the more she could escape the parts of herself she couldn't bear to confront. But the truth was, the more she ran, the less she knew who she really was.

"I don't know if I can face it," Isabelle whispered, looking down at her hands, the sand now slipping through her fingers. "What if I'm not the person I want to be? What if I've been running from something that I can't escape? What if I'm just... lost?"

Alex reached out, his hand gently touching her arm. "You're not lost. You're just scared. And that's okay. It's okay to be scared. But you can't let fear control you. You have the power to decide what comes next. Not your family. Not anyone else. You."

Isabelle's heart pounded in her chest as she turned to face him fully. The depth in his eyes, the sincerity in his voice, made something inside her shift. She had spent so much time hiding from herself, from her past, from the weight of the Stone name. But Alex was right. She couldn't keep running. Not from herself, and not from her past.

The reality of the situation hit her like a tidal wave. She had been so focused on escaping that she hadn't stopped to think about what she was running toward. Was this life—this free-spirited existence she had created for herself—really what she wanted? Or had it simply been a temporary solution, a way to avoid the uncomfortable truths she wasn't ready to face?

She looked at Alex, the man who had shown her a different way of seeing the world, a way of living that didn't require pretense or the weight of legacy. But could she really embrace that life? Could she truly walk away from everything she had known, from the empire that was her birthright, and live a life that was completely her own?

"I don't know what to do," she said, her voice breaking as she fought to hold back the emotions welling up inside her. "I don't know if I can face them. I don't know if I can face the life they want me to lead. I'm scared, Alex. I'm scared of what it will mean if I choose this new life. I'm scared of what I'll lose."

Alex's expression softened even more, and Isabelle saw the

vulnerability in his eyes for the first time. "You're not alone in this, Isabelle," he said gently. "You don't have to figure everything out right now. But whatever you decide, just know that it's your decision. It's your life. You have the power to choose."

For a moment, the weight of his words settled over her like a heavy blanket. Isabelle stood there, her feet buried in the sand, staring out at the horizon as the last light of day disappeared beneath the waves. She didn't know what the future held, didn't know if she was ready to leap, but something had shifted in her. The fear that had been choking her for so long began to ease, replaced by a flicker of hope, however tiny.

"I don't know if I'm ready," she whispered. "But I know I can't keep running."

Alex gave her a small, encouraging smile. "Then you've already taken the first step."

They stood in silence, the wind whispering through the trees around them, the sound of the waves a steady, calming presence in the background. Isabelle had no answers yet, no clear path forward. But for the first time in a long time, she felt like she was standing on the edge of something new—something real. And maybe, just maybe, that was enough.

The evening stretched on, and Isabelle felt a shift in herself. She didn't have all the answers, but she had started the journey toward finding them. And for the first time in a long time, that was enough.

She turned back toward the path that led to the small village where they had been staying. It was time to stop running. Time to face what she had been avoiding.

And with that thought, a sense of peace washed over her, quiet and profound. She wasn't lost. She was starting to find herself.

Six

The Ties That Bind

The days since their discovery of the wooden box in the jungle temple had been uneventful on the surface. Isabelle—Izzy Bloom—had returned to the life she had tried so desperately to create, photographing the vibrant streets and quiet corners of the city, capturing fleeting moments of beauty that seemed to exist only for her. But something had shifted. There was an unsettling tension that had settled in the pit of her stomach, a feeling she couldn't escape, as though the discovery had unleashed a ripple effect that was slowly but surely threatening to pull her back into a life she had left behind.

It wasn't just the box—though that alone was enough to gnaw at her. It was the way Alex had become distant, as though he, too, had felt the subtle shift in the air. For days, they had continued their explorations, but their conversations had become strained, their once-easy camaraderie now laden with an unspoken tension that neither of them seemed able to address. Isabelle had tried to shake the feeling, telling herself that everything was fine, that she was still in control of her new life. But deep down, she knew she wasn't.

The more she thought about it, the more she realized that it wasn't just the box that troubled her—it was the way Alex had handled it. The intensity in his eyes when he insisted they take it with them had unsettled her, though she hadn't said anything at the time. It was as if the box had become a symbol of something greater, something neither of them understood. And the more time passed, the more Isabelle felt herself being drawn into whatever web Alex was weaving—whether he knew it or not.

She had spent the better part of the morning wandering the streets, trying to lose herself in the crowd. The air was thick with humidity, the city alive with the chaotic energy of the midday rush. People bustled about, unaware of the unease that had crept into Isabelle's chest, but she couldn't shake it. Her phone had been silent all morning, and she knew why. Her family was looking for her. They had to be.

Her father's lawyer had called again last night, the voicemail almost pleading, and a few texts from her assistant had gone unanswered. The messages were always polite, always framed as concerned inquiries about her well-being, but Isabelle could hear the underlying panic in their tone. Her absence had become a problem—a problem that needed to be solved, not for her sake, but for the sake of the Stone Hotel legacy.

As much as Isabelle had tried to break free, she knew that

her family's ties were not so easily severed. They were, quite literally, in her blood. The Stone name carried weight, not just in the business world, but in every facet of her life. She had always been the perfect heiress, the perfect daughter, the perfect image of success. Now, with each day she spent hiding, her family's expectations felt more like chains, pulling her back toward a life she had no desire to return to.

She paused at a street corner, watching as the world passed by. She had come so far, and yet it felt like she was standing still, trapped between two realities. The one she had left behind, and the one she was trying to create.

Her phone buzzed in her pocket, and she immediately froze. She recognized the number on the screen. It was her father's lawyer.

Taking a deep breath, Isabelle answered the call. "Hello?"

"Ms. Stone," the voice on the other end said, cool and professional, but with an undercurrent of urgency. "I trust you're well, but we need to discuss your next steps. The board is growing increasingly concerned about your absence. Your father insists on hearing from you."

The mention of her father made Isabelle's stomach churn. "I've told you before, I'm fine," she said, trying to sound calm, trying to suppress the anxiety creeping up her throat. "I'm just taking a break, like I said."

The lawyer's voice softened, but it wasn't the softness of

understanding—it was the softness of someone who had grown accustomed to handling the delicate negotiations of the wealthy. "I understand, Ms. Stone. But the company cannot continue without your direct involvement. Your father is prepared to meet with you. Please let us know when you'll return."

The silence that followed was thick with expectation. Isabelle could hear the urgency in his voice, the unspoken threat. Her absence was no longer a minor inconvenience; it was a problem that needed to be fixed. The Stone Hotel empire needed her. They always needed her.

"I'm not coming back yet," Isabelle said, her voice steady, though her heart was racing. "I need more time."

"Of course," the lawyer said, his tone tight. "But please, we urge you to reconsider. Your father insists on a meeting."

"I'll think about it," Isabelle said, ending the call without waiting for a response.

She stood still for a moment, the weight of her family's expectations pressing down on her like a physical force. Every time she thought she had a handle on her new life, it was like they found a way to pull her back.

With a sigh, she slipped her phone back into her pocket and resumed walking, trying to push the conversation from her mind. But even as she walked, she couldn't shake the feeling that the call had been a warning—a reminder that she wasn't really free. Not yet.

As the evening drew near, Isabelle found herself back at the café where she and Alex had spent hours talking just days earlier. It was quieter now, the sun sinking low in the sky, casting long shadows across the street. She could see him sitting at the same table, his camera resting beside him as he stared out at the street, deep in thought.

"Alex," Isabelle called, her voice barely louder than a whisper.

He turned at the sound of her voice, his eyes meeting hers, and for a moment, she thought she saw something—something that wasn't there before. A flicker of recognition, perhaps, or maybe a quiet understanding. His expression softened as she approached, and he gestured for her to sit.

"You're quiet tonight," he said, his voice gentle, almost knowing.

Isabelle shrugged, sitting down across from him. "I've just been thinking a lot."

"About what?" Alex asked, leaning forward slightly. "You've been distant. You've been off ever since we found the box."

Isabelle hesitated, unsure how to articulate the turmoil swirling inside her. "It's not just the box. It's everything. I feel… trapped, Alex. I thought I could escape, but it's like I can't get away from it. The past keeps finding me, no matter how far I run."

Alex's eyes softened, and for a moment, he seemed to consider her words carefully. "You know, sometimes running isn't the answer," he said quietly. "Sometimes you have to face what you're running from. You can't outrun your past forever."

The words stung more than she expected. She looked away, trying to steady herself. "I don't know if I'm ready for that. I don't even know what I'm supposed to face."

Alex didn't respond immediately. Instead, he reached into his bag and pulled out the wooden box, placing it on the table between them. Isabelle's breath caught in her throat. She hadn't expected to see it again. She had hoped, perhaps, that it would be forgotten, lost to time and the jungle that had hidden it.

"We need to talk about this," Alex said, his voice low and serious. "It's not just a box, Isabelle. It's something more. I can feel it. And I think you can, too."

Isabelle swallowed hard, staring at the box as though it might suddenly come to life. "What do you mean?" she asked, her voice barely audible.

Alex met her gaze, his expression intense. "I think we've both uncovered something bigger than we can handle. Something that neither of us fully understands. But we need to figure it out, or it's going to keep pulling us both in."

Isabelle felt the weight of his words settle over her. The ties that bound her to her past, to her family, to the life she had thought she could escape—those same ties were now pulling her toward something much darker. And this time, there would be no running away. Not without facing the truth.

Seven

The Shattered Facade

Isabelle's footsteps echoed in the quiet hallway as she made her way back to her room. The cool air of the hotel's dimly lit corridor did little to quell the suffocating pressure that had settled in her chest since the conversation with Alex. The weight of his words hung over her like an invisible storm cloud, dark and looming, ready to burst open. She couldn't ignore it any longer. The secrets they had uncovered—the box, the mysterious energy surrounding it—had already begun to unravel her carefully constructed life. And for the first time in weeks, Isabelle felt like she was standing on the precipice of something she wasn't ready to face.

She reached her door, her hand trembling slightly as she slid the keycard into the slot. The door clicked open, and she stepped inside, the familiar scent of antiseptic and polished wood immediately enveloping her. But nothing felt familiar anymore. Not her room, not her life. Everything was shifting beneath her feet.

Her phone buzzed in her pocket, and Isabelle paused, the knot in her stomach tightening as she pulled it out. The screen displayed her father's lawyer's number. Her heart skipped a beat. She had known this call was coming, but it didn't make it any easier. With a deep breath, she answered it.

"Ms. Stone," the voice on the other end was smooth, but there was an edge to it that sent a chill through her. "I trust you're well. Your father is still very concerned about your whereabouts. He insists on meeting with you. You're needed at home, Isabelle. The board is growing restless. Your absence is becoming more than a mere inconvenience."

Isabelle closed her eyes, feeling the sharp sting of her father's demands pierce through her. She had hoped—no, prayed— that she could escape for a little longer, that she could carve out some space for herself before being dragged back into the world of duty and responsibility. But it seemed that her family's grip was stronger than she had hoped. They had never let go, not really. And now, it was only a matter of time before they pulled her back into their fold.

"I'm not coming back yet," she said, her voice steady despite the rising panic in her chest. "I need more time."

"I understand," the lawyer replied, his tone turning cold. "But I urge you to reconsider. Your father has made it clear that he won't wait much longer. This meeting is no longer optional,

Isabelle."

The words hung in the air, heavy and suffocating. Isabelle's jaw clenched as she fought to keep her composure. She couldn't let her family dictate her every move anymore. She couldn't go back. Not now, not after everything she had learned, after everything she had uncovered about herself. But the truth was, she had no idea what would happen if she didn't return. The consequences were uncharted territory, and the fear of what might come next gnawed at her like a slow-burning fire.

"I'll think about it," Isabelle said, her voice hardening. "I'll call you when I'm ready."

The line went silent for a moment before the lawyer responded. "Of course. But don't take too long, Isabelle. Time is running out."

The call ended abruptly, and Isabelle stood frozen for a moment, the weight of the conversation settling over her like a thick fog. She felt trapped, pulled in two opposite directions—her family's expectations and the life she was trying to build with Alex. Her chest tightened as she realized how much she had invested in this new life, this illusion of freedom. Could she really give it all up and return to the cold, sterile world of her family's empire? Could she continue pretending to be Izzy Bloom, the carefree traveler, when everything around her was starting to collapse?

With a shaky breath, Isabelle sank onto the edge of the bed, her thoughts racing. She knew she couldn't keep running, not forever. But the thought of facing her family again—of stepping back into the role they had crafted for her—felt like a death sentence. It was everything she had tried to escape. And now, the past was calling her back, with a vengeance.

She jumped at the sound of a knock on the door.

"Come in," she called out, her voice strained.

The door creaked open, and Alex stepped into the room, his eyes scanning the space as though looking for something. He hadn't seen her since their conversation earlier in the day, and there was a noticeable distance between them now. The easy camaraderie they had once shared seemed like a distant memory.

"Is everything okay?" Alex asked, his voice low, his gaze soft with concern.

Isabelle hesitated, her mind still reeling from the call. She could feel the words pressing against her chest, but she didn't know how to explain it to him. Could she even explain it? He had no idea what her family had put her through, how they had shaped her entire existence around their own needs and desires. He couldn't possibly understand the kind of pressure she was under.

"I… I just got off the phone with my father's lawyer," Isabelle said, her voice barely above a whisper. "They want me to come back. They say the board's getting impatient. It's… it's becoming impossible to ignore."

Alex remained silent for a moment, his eyes locked on hers. There was no judgment, no harsh words. Just quiet understanding. But Isabelle couldn't escape the feeling that he knew more than she was letting on. He had seen her struggle with her past, with her identity, and he wasn't letting her off the hook. Not this time.

"You have to face them, Isabelle," Alex said softly, his voice steady but firm. "You can't keep running from your family, from your past. You can't keep pretending to be someone you're not."

The words hit her like a slap, and she recoiled, her heart thumping painfully in her chest. It was too much—too much for her to process in one moment. Her family, Alex, the box, the pressure—it was all converging in one overwhelming tidal wave, and she didn't know how to swim.

"I'm not running," she snapped, more harshly than she intended. "I'm just… I'm just trying to figure out who I am. Is that so hard to understand?"

Alex stepped closer, his expression softening, but there was something in his eyes that made Isabelle freeze. It was a kind of raw honesty she hadn't expected.

"I understand more than you think," Alex said quietly. "You think running away will solve everything. But it won't. It'll just leave you more broken than you were before."

Isabelle opened her mouth to protest, but the words caught in her throat. He was right. She knew it, deep down. She had been running her whole life—running from her responsibilities, from her family's expectations, from the person they had wanted her to be. But the truth was, she had no idea who she was without them. Who was Isabelle Stone if she wasn't the heir to the Stone Hotel empire? Who was Izzy Bloom, the traveler, the wanderer? Did she even know anymore?

The weight of his words settled in the pit of her stomach, and Isabelle felt herself unraveling. She didn't want to face the truth, not yet. Not when everything she had worked for—the life she had so carefully built—was slipping away like sand through her fingers.

"Maybe it's time you face what you're really running from," Alex said, his voice low, almost a whisper. "The truth is, you're not running from your family. You're running from yourself. You're trying to hide from what you really want, what you really need."

Isabelle's breath caught in her throat. She wanted to push him away, to deny the truth he was speaking, but deep down, she knew he was right.

Her phone buzzed again, cutting through the silence. She glanced at the screen, her heart pounding when she saw the name on the caller ID.

Her father's lawyer.

For a moment, she just stared at it, the weight of the decision pressing down on her. She could feel the ties pulling her back toward the life she had escaped. The luxury, the power, the expectations—all of it waiting for her to come back. But what would it cost her? What would it cost her to continue playing the role they had written for her?

With a trembling hand, Isabelle silenced the call, her finger lingering on the screen as she fought to steady her breathing.

"I have to make a decision," she said, her voice trembling. "But I don't know what to do anymore."

Alex didn't say anything. He just reached out, his hand resting gently on her arm. And for the first time in weeks, Isabelle felt something shift within her. It wasn't an answer, but it was a beginning.

The ties that had bound her to her past were still there. But now, she had to decide whether to break them or let them consume her.

Eight

Crisis of Conscience

The morning light filtered through the cracked blinds, casting long, slanted shadows across the room. Isabelle stood at the window, her eyes tracing the motion of the busy street below. The city was alive, the sounds of motorbikes and street vendors filling the air with an energy she used to embrace. But today, it all felt distant, as though she were watching a world that no longer belonged to her. Her phone lay forgotten on the bed, the screen dark, but she could feel its weight—its unspoken demand.

Alex's words from the night before echoed in her mind, stirring up emotions she had spent so long burying. You're running from yourself. They had struck her with a force she hadn't expected, exposing something deep within her that she had long ignored. She had been running. From her family, from her responsibilities, from a life that had been carefully crafted for her. But in the process, she had lost sight of who she really was.

She glanced at the phone again, her stomach tightening. The missed calls from her father's lawyer were like little marks on a map, drawing her back to a life she couldn't escape, no matter how far she ran. And now, the decision weighed heavily on her—should she continue hiding, continue pretending to be someone she wasn't? Or was it time to face the life she had left behind and finally deal with the mess she had created?

She had no answers. And worse, she didn't know where to start looking for them.

The knock at the door startled her. She glanced at the clock on the wall—midday. Alex had left early that morning for a photo shoot, leaving her alone with her thoughts, her fears, and the lingering tension between them. She had expected solitude, but now, with the knock, she felt a fresh wave of dread wash over her.

"Coming," Isabelle called, walking toward the door with a slow, deliberate pace. As she opened it, she wasn't surprised to find Alex standing there, his face tight with an unreadable expression.

"I thought we needed to talk," he said, stepping into the room without waiting for an invitation. His eyes searched hers, a quiet intensity in them. There was no smile, no warm greeting. Just the weight of his gaze, as if he were waiting for her to reveal something she hadn't yet said.

Isabelle closed the door behind him, swallowing the lump that had formed in her throat. She had been expecting this, yet she wasn't ready for it. There was something about the way Alex looked at her now that made her feel exposed, like all of her hidden fears and regrets were laid bare for him to see.

"I… I don't know what to say," she began, her voice faltering. "I've been thinking about everything you said last night. About facing my family. About facing myself."

Alex didn't interrupt her, but his eyes never left her face, his jaw set tight in a way that told her he wasn't just waiting for her to speak. He was waiting for her to make a decision, to confront the truth that had been circling them both like a predator waiting for the right moment to strike.

"I don't know if I'm ready to go back," she continued, her voice shaking now. "I'm not sure I can do it. To return to the life I left behind. To step back into that world where I was always someone else, someone they needed me to be."

Alex stepped closer, his presence suddenly overwhelming. He reached out, placing his hand on hers, grounding her. "Isabelle," he said softly, his voice almost a whisper, "you don't have to go back. Not if you don't want to. But you do need to stop running. You need to stop hiding from the truth."

Isabelle felt a pang of guilt, a tight knot in her chest. She wasn't sure whether it was guilt for wanting to escape her past or guilt for leaning on Alex in ways that felt like betrayal to herself. She had trusted him, trusted his vision of a life free from the chains of her family's influence. But now, as the reality of her situation settled in, she realized she was asking him to be something he couldn't be—her salvation, her escape.

"I don't know who I am without them, Alex," she said, her voice barely above a whisper. "Without the expectations, without the legacy. All I've ever known is what they wanted me to be. And now, I don't even know if I can live outside of that."

Alex's hand tightened around hers, his voice low and steady. "Then it's time to find out. You've been running from yourself for so long, Isabelle. Maybe it's time you stopped. Maybe it's time you discovered who you are when no one else is telling you who to be."

Her breath caught in her throat, and she pulled her hand away from his, stepping back. His words felt too real, too cutting. She had wanted freedom, wanted escape, but the price of that freedom was becoming clearer by the minute. If she continued down this path, there would be no turning back. She would have to confront her past, confront her family—and confront herself. She wasn't sure if she was ready for that. The truth was, she wasn't sure if she ever would be.

"I can't do it," she muttered, shaking her head. "I can't go back to them. I can't go back to that life. I just… I don't know what's left for me if I don't."

Alex stood still, watching her with a quiet intensity that made Isabelle's pulse race. He was waiting, his patience unwavering. He wasn't pushing her, wasn't rushing her. But she could feel the weight of his gaze, as though he knew something she didn't—something she wasn't ready to face.

"I know you're scared," he said softly. "But you can't keep running forever. You need to choose, Isabelle. You need to decide what kind of life you want to live. And you need to start living it, not just hiding from it."

The silence between them stretched for what felt like an eternity. Isabelle's mind spun, torn between the comfort of the life she had known—the world of her family's wealth and power—and the strange, dangerous allure of the freedom she had begun to taste. But was it freedom? Or was it just another illusion, another version of the same facade she had been living for years?

"I can't choose," Isabelle whispered, the words slipping from her lips before she could stop them. "I'm not sure there's a choice anymore."

Alex stepped toward her, his voice firm, though still gentle. "You have to choose, Isabelle. The longer you stay in limbo, the more of yourself you lose. Your family won't give you the life you want. They'll just keep pulling you back into their web. But you have the power to break free. You always have."

Isabelle's heart thundered in her chest, her body trembling with the weight of the decision before her. She had always been a prisoner to her family's desires, a pawn in their game of legacy and control. But for the first time, Alex was offering her a way out. A way to be her own person, to decide her own future. It wasn't a promise of comfort, of safety. But it was a chance—a chance to choose herself, to find the courage to confront her fears and step into a life of her own making.

But was she strong enough? Could she really do it? Or would she crumble under the weight of her family's expectations, under the pressure of a life that had been mapped out for her long before she was born?

The decision loomed, and Isabelle felt the tension in her chest tighten, suffocating her. She looked at Alex, his face a mixture of concern and quiet encouragement, and for the first time in what felt like forever, she saw a glimmer of something—something that wasn't tied to her family, to her legacy, or to the life she had been forced to live. It was freedom. Raw and terrifying, but real.

With a shaky breath, Isabelle made a choice. She didn't know if it was the right one. She didn't know if she was ready. But for the first time, she was choosing herself.

"I'll face them," she said, her voice strong, though it trembled with the weight of her decision. "I'll go back. But on my terms. Not theirs."

Alex's expression softened, and for a moment, Isabelle saw the quiet pride in his eyes. He didn't say anything—he didn't need to. The choice had been made.

And for the first time in a long time, Isabelle felt the tiniest spark of hope flicker inside her, as if, maybe, just maybe, she could still find her way out of the web her family had trapped her in.

But the road ahead would be long—and the consequences of her choice would be far from easy.

The Road to Redemption

The morning after Isabelle's decision to return to her family felt oddly calm. The quiet weight of it pressed down on her as she walked through the bustling streets of the city. She had barely slept the night before, her mind racing with the implications of the choice she had made. The idea of stepping back into the world of the Stone Hotel empire, of facing her father and the family that had always kept her tethered, filled her with a mixture of dread and resolve. She knew the road ahead wouldn't be easy, but she had made her choice. She was no longer running.

Alex's words from last night lingered in her mind as she moved through the crowded streets, the air thick with the usual heat and noise. The longer you stay in limbo, the more of yourself you lose. It had been a simple statement, but it had struck her to the core. How many years had she spent in limbo? Hiding behind a facade of wealth, privilege, and power, too afraid to confront the reality of who she was beneath it all? Too afraid to face the demands of a family that would never let her go?

Her thoughts were interrupted by a soft buzz from her phone. She glanced down, her heart sinking when she saw the caller ID. Her father's lawyer. The call she had been dreading.

Taking a deep breath, Isabelle answered the phone, trying to steady the tremble in her voice. "Hello?"

"Ms. Stone," the lawyer's voice was crisp and professional, but there was a layer of urgency beneath it that made Isabelle's stomach tighten. "Your father is expecting your return. He insists on meeting with you at your earliest convenience. The board has been informed of your decision, and they're eager to discuss the future of Stone Hotels."

Isabelle closed her eyes, feeling a wave of panic crash over her. She hadn't realized how quickly everything would move. How quickly they would pull her back into the fold.

"I'm on my way," she said, trying to sound more confident than she felt. "Please tell him I'll be there shortly."

The lawyer's response was a terse, "We'll be waiting, Ms. Stone," before the call ended.

Isabelle looked around at the chaos of the street—vendors shouting, people rushing by in every direction—and felt the strange sense of isolation that always came when she had to face her father's world. She had thought she could stay away, build a life separate from the expectations they had placed on her. But now, it felt like she was being pulled back into a vortex she couldn't escape, and the more she fought it, the more she realized how little control she had.

Her phone buzzed again, this time a message from Alex.

Good luck, Isabelle. Whatever happens, you've already shown courage. Take it one step at a time.

Her fingers hovered over the screen for a moment before she put the phone back in her pocket. Alex's words were comforting, but they didn't erase the storm that was brewing inside her. She wasn't sure if she was making the right choice, but the truth was, she wasn't sure what the right choice even looked like anymore.

The ride to the Stone family mansion felt like it took an eternity. The streets outside the taxi window blurred as Isabelle tried to steady her breathing. The familiar grandeur of the mansion, the sprawling estate that had always been a symbol of the Stone legacy, loomed ahead, and with it, all the memories of her childhood—memories of being groomed to take over the empire, memories of never being allowed to make a choice for herself, of always being told who to be, what to want, and how to behave.

She had left it all behind, but it seemed that no matter how far she ran, it always found her.

The taxi pulled up to the grand entrance of the mansion, and

Isabelle hesitated before stepping out. The air was thick with tension, and her heartbeat pounded in her ears. She couldn't afford to be weak now, not when she had already made the hardest decision of her life.

The door opened with a soft creak as Isabelle stepped into the foyer. The marble floors gleamed under the light of crystal chandeliers, and the scent of fresh flowers hung in the air. It was all so familiar, so cold. Everything about this place screamed control, tradition, and the unrelenting weight of family legacy.

"Isabelle," a voice called from the top of the grand staircase.

Her father stood at the top, his figure imposing, dressed in a perfectly tailored suit that fit him as though he had just stepped out of a magazine. He was the epitome of power and authority, the man who had built the Stone Hotel empire from the ground up. But to Isabelle, he was nothing more than a stranger who had molded her into a version of himself that she could never live up to. His eyes were sharp, assessing, and as always, there was no warmth in them, only expectation.

She forced a smile, lifting her chin as she climbed the stairs to meet him. She could feel his gaze on her, weighing her, as though he could see through the veil of her disguise, see the cracks in the facade she had built.

"You're late," her father said curtly as she reached the top of the stairs.

"I'm here now," Isabelle replied, her voice steady despite the tension gnawing at her insides.

Her father gave a single nod, his lips curling into a thin smile that didn't reach his eyes. "Good. We have a lot to discuss. Follow me."

He turned without waiting for her to respond, and Isabelle followed him into the grand office at the far end of the mansion. The room was bathed in the warm glow of sunlight streaming through the large windows, but it felt cold. The walls were lined with bookshelves, each shelf neatly organized with leather-bound books, awards, and plaques that spoke to the family's legacy. The desk was large and polished, made of dark wood that gleamed under the light. Everything in the room exuded control, success, and the weight of history. But for Isabelle, it felt suffocating.

Her father gestured for her to sit, and she did so, her back straight, her hands folded in her lap.

"I assume you've had time to think about your position," he said, his tone sharp as he seated himself behind the desk. "Your absence has caused a ripple, Isabelle. The board is beginning to lose faith in your ability to lead this company. Your sudden disappearance was… unprofessional."

Isabelle's stomach churned at the words. She had known this was coming, but hearing it from him—hearing it from her father, the man who had shaped her entire life—was a blow she hadn't been prepared for.

"I'm sorry for any inconvenience my absence has caused," she said, her voice steady, though it felt like a lie. "But I'm here now, and I'm ready to move forward."

Her father's eyes narrowed slightly, as if searching for something in her expression. "You say that now, but can you really step back into your role as CEO of Stone Hotels? Can you really handle the pressure that comes with it? Or do you think you can live a quiet life outside of this company, pretending to be someone else?"

The words stung, more than she had anticipated. Isabelle had spent so long trying to escape this very pressure, trying to prove that she was more than the legacy of the Stone family. But now, sitting in front of her father, she felt the weight of those expectations pressing down on her once again. He had never believed in her ability to make her own choices, to be her own person. To him, she was just a tool—an heir to the empire, nothing more.

"I'm not pretending to be someone else," Isabelle said, her voice harder now, more defiant. "I'm trying to figure out who I am, not just what you want me to be."

Her father's eyes flashed with irritation. "This is about the company, Isabelle. Not your 'self-discovery.' You've been given everything. All of this," he gestured around the room, "is yours. And yet, you've chosen to abandon it."

Isabelle's breath quickened. She had never felt more suffocated in her life. She could feel the walls closing in on her, could feel herself slipping back into the role she had been assigned so many years ago. But something inside her snapped. She couldn't keep doing this. Not for him. Not for anyone.

"I didn't abandon anything," she said, her voice trembling with raw emotion. "I was never given the chance to choose for myself. I was never given the chance to figure out what I want. I've spent my whole life doing what you and the board wanted. But I'm done, Father. I'm done being who you want me to be."

Her father's face darkened, his jaw clenched with barely contained rage. "You will regret this," he said, his voice low and threatening.

Isabelle met his gaze, unflinching. "Maybe. But at least I'll be living my own life."

For the first time, she felt a flicker of freedom—small, fragile, but undeniably hers. The weight of her family's expectations hadn't disappeared, but now, she had the courage to face them head-on. She had chosen herself, and that was a victory she wasn't willing to forfeit.

Her father's eyes burned with anger, but Isabelle stood her ground. The road to redemption had just begun, but it was a road she was ready to walk, no matter the cost.

And as she left the mansion that day, Isabelle knew one thing for sure: the journey ahead wouldn't be easy. But for the first time in her life, she was truly free.

Ten

Breaking Free

The sun barely rose when Isabelle stepped out of the taxi and into the cold, sterile world she had left behind. The sprawling Stone Hotel complex loomed before her, its towering glass walls and sleek metal exterior a testament to her family's dominance in the luxury industry. Everything about the building screamed control, power, and wealth. The marble floors, the polished elevators, the state-of-the-art technology—it was all designed to remind her that the Stone legacy could never be escaped, not indeed.

She hesitated for a moment, standing on the sidewalk outside the entrance. Her heart thudded painfully, and she fought to steady her breath. This was it—the moment she had been dreading for weeks. The moment she would face her family, her father, and the life she had tried to escape.

But today was different. She wasn't the same Isabelle Stone who had left this world behind in search of something better. She wasn't the same woman who had allowed her family to dictate her every move. Today, she was Izzy Bloom. Today, she was someone who had made her own choices and had the strength to live by them, no matter the consequences.

She looked around one last time, her eyes taking in the city she had grown to love during her time away. The quiet hum of the early morning was familiar, but now, it felt like a world apart from the life she had been born into. The contrast between the two was almost jarring. There was no luxury here, no finely tailored suits or polished floors. Just the simplicity of the streets, the bustling people going about their day.

Taking a deep breath, Isabelle walked through the hotel's revolving doors and into the heart of the empire she had tried to distance herself from. The lobby was as pristine and imposing as ever. The polished marble floors gleamed under the bright lights, and the sleek, modern furnishings stood in sharp contrast to the antique decor of her childhood home. She had grown up in this space, surrounded by the clamor of business meetings, staff hustling around her, and the hum of the ever-present machine that was Stone Hotels.

But none of that mattered now. She wasn't here to be the dutiful heir, the poised daughter who played her part in the family's grand design. She wasn't here to smile for the cameras or make polite conversation with the board members. No. Isabelle was here to face the truth. She was here to confront the man who had shaped her life—and to take control of her future.

The elevator ride to her father's office felt like an eternity. The familiar sound of the soft chime as the floors ticked by only reminded her of how much time had passed, how much she had tried to outrun. The elevator door opened with a soft whoosh, and Isabelle stepped out into the long hallway that led to the executive offices. She was no longer a child, no longer the heir who had been groomed to inherit the empire. She was a woman who had been through too much to turn back now.

Her father's office was at the end of the hall, behind a set of double doors that seemed to loom ahead, waiting to swallow her whole. With each step, her heart pounded harder in her chest. Her body felt heavy, as if the weight of everything—the expectations, the promises, the legacy—was pressing down on her. She had spent so many years trying to live up to those expectations, trying to please him, trying to be who he wanted her to be. But that wasn't her anymore.

She reached for the doorknob, her hand trembling for just a moment before she steadied it, and pushed the doors open.

Her father sat behind his desk, his back straight, his hands folded in front of him. He didn't look up as she entered, his eyes focused on the papers in front of him. The air between them was thick with years of unspoken tension, of words that had never been said, of feelings that had never been acknowledged. He didn't even greet her. He simply waited.

Isabelle stepped inside, closing the door quietly behind her. She could feel his eyes on her now, assessing, calculating. She stood there for a moment, gathering her thoughts, her resolve. There was no turning back now.

"You're late," he said, his voice as cold and dismissive as ever.

"I'm here," Isabelle replied, her voice steady. "And I've made my decision."

Her father raised an eyebrow, the corner of his mouth curling into the smallest of smirks. "Have you? After all this time, you've finally come to your senses?"

Isabelle clenched her fists at her sides. She couldn't let him undermine her, not this time. "I've come to my senses," she said, her voice firm. "But not in the way you think."

Her father leaned back in his chair, his fingers tapping rhythmically on the desk. "I hope you've learned the importance of responsibility. Of doing what's right for the company. Your absence has caused quite a stir, Isabelle. You've made a spectacle of yourself."

"I've made a spectacle of myself?" Isabelle echoed, her anger bubbling to the surface. "You've never once asked me what I wanted, what I needed. You've spent my whole life making decisions for me, controlling every aspect of my existence. But not anymore."

Her father's eyes flashed with annoyance. "You don't understand, Isabelle. This company, this family—it's everything. Your responsibility to it is paramount."

"Not anymore," Isabelle said, her voice rising with emotion. "I've spent my life being what you wanted me to be. But I can't do that anymore. I've tried to live up to your expectations, to be the perfect daughter, the perfect heir. But I can't. And I won't."

Her father's face hardened. "So, what is this? A rebellion? You think you can just walk away from everything we've built? This company is your legacy. You're throwing it all away for what? Some fantasy life that has no foundation?"

"No," Isabelle said, her voice unwavering. "I'm not throwing anything away. I'm finding myself. I'm choosing a life where I don't have to live under the shadow of your expectations. I'm choosing a life where I get to make my own decisions, live my own way. I don't need your approval anymore."

There was a long silence, broken only by the sound of her father's breathing. His face was unreadable, his eyes hard and calculating, as though he were weighing his next move. Isabelle held her breath, bracing herself for whatever words might come next.

"You are making a mistake," he said finally, his voice low and dangerous. "You think you can escape this. You think you can just walk away from everything we've worked for. But you can't. This company is yours, Isabelle. You are the heir. There's no getting away from it."

"I don't want to be the heir," Isabelle said, her voice calm but resolute. "I want to be me. And that's not something you can give me. You've spent my whole life trying to make me into something I'm not. But I can't do it anymore."

Her father's eyes narrowed, his fists clenched at his sides. "If you think you can simply walk away from this family, from this company, you're gravely mistaken. You're throwing away everything. Your birthright. Your future."

"My future?" Isabelle repeated, her voice thick with emotion. "This isn't my future. Not anymore. You don't get to decide that for me."

For a moment, her father said nothing. He stared at her, the anger in his eyes burning with intensity. Then, slowly, he stood up from his chair, towering over her.

"You will regret this, Isabelle," he said, his voice a low growl. "You will regret walking away from everything we've built. And when you come crawling back, begging for forgiveness, remember this moment."

Isabelle stood her ground, refusing to back down. "I'm not crawling back. I'm leaving, Father. And I'm not looking back."

There was a flicker of something in her father's eyes for the first time—something that wasn't anger or control but something darker. "You think you're free," he said, his voice quiet, almost a whisper. "But you'll find that freedom comes with a price."

Isabelle didn't answer. She didn't need to. She turned on her heel and walked out of the office, her heart pounding. The doors slammed behind her with a finality that echoed through the grand hallway, and Isabelle felt something inside her—something that had been buried for years—finally snap into place.

She was free.

But she wasn't naïve. She knew that the price of her freedom wouldn't come easily. Her family would fight to pull her back, to drag her into the world she had spent so long running from. But no matter the cost, Isabelle was done being who they wanted her to be. She had found herself, and no one—no matter how powerful—could take that away from her.

The road ahead would be difficult. There would be moments of doubt, moments when she would wonder if she had made the right choice. But Isabelle had crossed a line she could never uncross. And for the first time in her life, she was living for herself. The journey had only just begun, but she was ready. She was free.